Christmas Stories

The Magic Christmas Tree

The Lost Christmas Present

The Nutcracker

The Story of Christmas

LORENZ BOOKS

The night before Christmas eve, the snow came. Huge snowflakes floated out of the sky and settled on the forest floor. Soon, it was white wherever you looked. In the morning, the squirrel children rushed to the window to see the snow. They were very surprised to see a Christmas tree standing there.

"Where did it come from?" asked Furtail.

"There are no footprints anywhere near," said Nibbles.

"It must have arrived by magic!" cried Baby Nutkin. They carried the tree inside and gave it the best place in the room. Together they all decorated the tree. By lunchtime it looked bright and festive.

You can help the squirrels to decorate the Magic Christmas Tree and their room by adding your stickers to this scene.

Later that day, Furtail went to add something of his own to the tree. It was a paper icicle.

"I wish I could see where the Snow Queen lives," he thought as he hung it on the tree.

As quick as a wish, Furtail found himself in a huge, airy hall. There sat the Snow Queen dressed in white, with jewels of ice and a sparkling crown.

"Ah," she said, "my special guest. Come and sit beside me."

Stalactites hung down from the ceiling, stalagmites rose up from the floor. A snow elf struck them gently so that they rang and filled the hall with beautiful music. Other elves danced. When the concert was over, the Snow Queen gave Furtail his own musical icicles, but before he could thank her, he found himself back home, beside the tree.

Here is Furtail in the Palace of Ice. You can add your stickers of the icicles, the ice-crown and the dancing snow elves.

Nibbles went to hang a striped candy cane on the tree,
tying it on with a ribbon. "I wonder if the magical Land
of Sugarcandy really exists?", she thought.

Suddenly, she looked around and found herself in a
wonderful landscape. The ground underneath her was a
mosaic of tiny shiny candies, and a winding path made of
chocolate fudge led to a fantastic castle made of candy fruits.

Nibbles went up the path to the magic castle, where laughing sugar fairies appeared to greet her. "Hello!" they cried. "Come and play with us!" They made her hold out her apron and filled it with chocolates, sugar canes and candies of all kinds. Then, as she was about to thank them, she found herself back at home.

Here is Nibbles in the wonderful Land of Sugarcandy. Add your stickers of the sugar fairies, candy canes, and other goodies.

Next, Father Squirrel went to hang little silver bells on the magic tree. They made a tinkling sound, just like the bells on a jester's cap. "It would be fun to be a Christmas jester, at a king's banquet!" he thought to himself.

Then, to his amazement, he found himself in a crowded banquet hall. Long tables were piled high with food and candles, and decorated with holly. There was a king and queen, and many knights. They were all laughing at him – and he saw that he was wearing a jester's cap, and had bells on his pointed shoes.

Father Squirrel did a dance, and everyone cheered. He juggled balls high in the air, and everyone clapped. He bowed low, to accept a gift from the king. When he stood up straight, he was back home again, and there were bells on his toes.

Here is Father Squirrel dancing at the banquet. You can complete the scene with your stickers of the juggling balls, the goblets, the plate of food and the sprig of holly.

Baby Nutkin looked inside his box of toys. He found a little wooden Santa. He tied a piece of cotton to it and hung it on the tree.

"I wish I could see where Santa lives," he thought, and then suddenly that's where he was: in a large workshop with long benches and piles of brightly wrapped presents. Elves were busy all around him.

Someone said: "Keep busy, over there!" So Nutkin joined in. He loaded presents into the sleigh and brushed the reindeer.

Santa said: "Thankyou for your help," and gave him six little packages.

Back home, Baby Nutkin put the packages beneath the tree and went to find his brother and sister.

Here you can see Santa's workshop. Use your stickers of the presents, the toys, the elves and their tools to complete the scene.

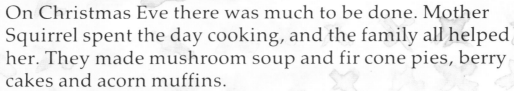

On Christmas Eve there was much to be done. Mother Squirrel spent the day cooking, and the family all helped her. They made mushroom soup and fir cone pies, berry cakes and acorn muffins.

Father Squirrel made paper chains to hang from the ceiling, and paper crackers. They would not go bang, so you had to say it yourself. The squirrels sang while they worked and when it all was finished, they danced into the room where the tree stood. "I hope we all have a lovely Christmas Day," they all said to each other.

Here you can see the family busy in the kitchen. You can help them by adding to the picture your stickers of the festive food and the decorations.

The children were up early on Christmas morning. They built a snow-squirrel, skated on the pond and had sled races before returning home to enjoy a grand Christmas feast together. Then it was time for the presents. Everyone scampered off and returned with their arms full of gifts.

Never had they had such wonderful presents. Baby Nutkin's parcels contained small wooden elves; Nibbles gave everyone a candy cane; Furtail handed out the musical icicles and Father Squirrel gave them all a bell each. Then Mother Squirrel came in from the kitchen with a special all-nut Christmas cake she had baked secretly.

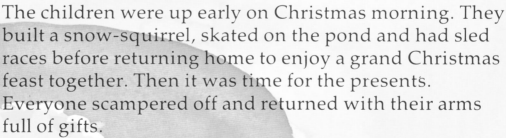

Here are the squirrels on Christmas day. You can complete the scene by adding your stickers of the presents.

Christmas was over and down came the decorations. No one wanted to part with the little tree, but Father Squirrel said it would be happier outside, as trees usually are.

The following day the Magic Christmas Tree had gone, and so had the snow. The forest floor stretched out before them, green and leafy. But where the tree had stood, there was a single white flower, the first of the year.

Add the squirrel's hats and other stickers to this final scene.

THE LOST CHRISTMAS PRESENT

One day, the postbear delivered something very exciting to the Brownlow Bears. It was a letter from their cousins, the Bearlaps. The Bearlaps were black bears and they lived far away in the Snowy Mountains.

"They want us to spend Christmas with them," said Mrs Brownlow. "Shall we go?" "Yes!" everyone replied.

"What an adventure it will be!" cried Mr Brownlow. "We'll need to start planning what presents to take them."

A few days before Christmas the Brownlows started packing for their holiday. They had a long way to go: across valleys and streams, through woods and meadows. Mrs Brownlow checked that her cubs had everything:

"Woolly scarfs? Snowboots? Toothbrushes? Book to read? Warm hats?" Billo and Fern nodded.

Mr Brownlow had more to carry than the others. He had a tent, a dozen maps, a small inflatable boat for crossing rivers, snowboots and a telescope. He struggled under the weight of it all.

They were just about to leave when Fern cried: "The presents!" They had forgotten the presents. She rushed back inside for them.

In this picture you can see the Brownlows packing for their holiday. You can help them by adding your stickers of the boots, the telescope, the maps, the book and the hats.

19

The Brownlows began their journey. Very soon, Mr Brownlow felt too hot. He grumbled about the weight of his bags while the others skipped on ahead.

By the end of the day, the bears were far away from the places they knew. They met new animals: an otter and chipmunks playing in the fresh snow.

As the sun set and the moon rose, they set up camp beside a river near some pine trees. Mr and Mrs Brownlow waded into the cold water to catch fish. The cubs went in search of firewood.

Here is the Brownlow's camp. You can complete the scene by adding your stickers of the fish jumping, chipmunks, the otter, the bags and the moon.

The Brownlows woke early the next morning. Mr Brownlow had not slept, he said, because of strange noises in the night. They set off. In a few hours they were there, beneath the Snowy Mountains.

"Good journey?" asked Mr Bearlap.

"Terrible," said Mr Brownlow, panting heavily. "It's a good thing I was well-prepared," and he dropped his heavy load to the ground with a sigh.

They were soon inside the Bearlaps' cosy den, unpacking their things. They put their toothbrushes on the shelf and their snowboots under the beds. But then they found that one of the presents was missing: the one for Mr Bearlap. Had they forgotten to pack it? Or had they lost it on the way?

Here are the bears unpacking their things. You can add your stickers of the cards and Christmas room decorations to complete the festive scene.

When he found out what had happened, Mr Bearlap said that they shouldn't worry.

"Christmas isn't just about presents," he said.

"You must have it! cried Mrs Brownlow, "I made it myself." So it was decided that they would all go and look for the lost present. They would retrace the Brownlow bears' steps through the forest. The bears split up so that they would have more chance of finding the present. It began to snow.

"Look out for grizzlies," said Mr Brownlow.

As he searched, Mr Bearlap wondered what the present might be. He hoped it would be a new scarf. He hoped it wasn't another sweater like the one that Mrs Brownlow had knitted him the year before. It had been much too big for him.

Here are the bears searching for the lost present. You can add your stickers of the map and all the other forest animals to the snowy scene.

The search party moved deeper into the forest. Then they heard a shout from Fern; she had found something. They all ran over to her, hoping it wasn't a grizzly, but she was pointing to something hanging from a branch. It was the red ribbon that had been around the present. Mr Bearlap put his paw to his lips and pointed to the mound of branches in front of them.

"Ssshh", he whispered. "It's a grizzly's den. Let's walk
away quietly."

But before they could tip-toe away, the door to the den
was thrown open and there before them stood the
largest and grizzliest grizzly bear they had ever
imagined.

"Happy Christmas!" he boomed. "Good of you to visit."

*Here you can see the grizzly bear coming out of his den. You can
add your stickers of the ribbon, the doorbell, Baby Bearlap, and
the forest birds and animals to the scene.*

Very nervously, the bears went inside the grizzly's den. The grizzly was in a very good mood. It was quite surprising.

"I am having a wonderful Christmas," said the grizzly bear. "You will never guess what has happened to me." The bears shook their heads. "Someone has given me a present," he continued. "A new sweater, and in just the right size!"

Then the bears all suddenly noticed that he was indeed wearing a new sweater, the one that Mrs Brownlow had made for Mr Bearlap. The grizzly twirled round for them to admire it.

"It suits you," said Mr Bearlap, and the others agreed that it looked very elegant.

Here is the scene inside the grizzly bear's home. You can complete the picture by adding to it your stickers of the things the bear has in his den.

The following day was Christmas day. Back in the Bearlaps' den everyone was busy and excited. Food was being prepared for dinner, and decorations were being added to the already bright and festive room. Mr Brownlow told the cubs that they would have to wait to open their presents, until their special guest arrived: the grizzly bear. He arrived looking larger than ever with his arms full of presents.

The cubs cheered and they all gathered around the Christmas tree. The grizzly bear handed a parcel to Mr Bearlap.

"What's this?" said the black bear, as he tore away the paper. "Ah" he smiled. "A new scarf. Just what I wanted."

Here are the bears opening their presents. You can complete the scene with your stickers of the gifts and the Christmas turkey.

31

A few days later it was time for the Brownlows to return to their own den. They packed their bags once more. Mr Brownlow looked at all the things he had brought with him and wondered if he had the strength to carry them all home again. He was delighted when the grizzly bear arrived and offered to help. They all waved goodbye to the Bearlaps and set off into the forest for the return trip home. It had been a wonderful Christmas.

Complete the final scene with your stickers of the handkerchief Mrs Bearlap is waving, the cub's snowman, and the forest animals who came to say goodbye.

THE NUTCRACKER

It's Christmas, most magical season of all,
And Clara and Fritz are dressing the tree.
Outside it is white from a recent snowfall,
But inside the fire crackles so merrily.

A knock at the door, the children clap hands,
The most special of guests has promised to call:
Their strange Uncle Drosselmeyer back from weird lands
Can be heard banging snow off his boots in the hall.

The welcomes and kisses are over and done;
A new cousin, Karl, so handsome, is met;
Now out come beautiful gifts one by one –
Each one appears more fantastical yet!

A huge clockwork mouse and a striped hobby horse;
For Clara some ballet shoes, glorious pink!
For young Fritz a team of toy soldiers, of course,
But what's in this last box they simply can't think . . .

Add your special festive stickers to the room.

A finely carved nutcracker doll dressed in red –
With a grimace so fierce even Fritz is afraid –
In the form of a soldier with plumes on its head,
And buttons and medals and all kinds of braid.

"It's called Kracko" says Drosselmeyer, seeing their joy,
"A Captain so brave, and now Clara's to own".
Young Fritz is so jealous he grabs at the toy,
And smashes it down (did I hear Kracko moan . . . ?)

When they'd done what they could to bandage his head,
When Fritz had said sorry – nearly polite –
They finally go upstairs tired-out to bed
But Clara is worried, and frets in the night.

Now place the stickers of all the other presents in the scene.

The brave little girl creeps down through the house
To comfort poor Kracko, lying so weak,
When suddenly out from the gloom rears a mouse,
At least six feet high, with a blood-curdling SQUEAK

The Mouse King cries "Slay the girl, she must die!"
And he signals his mouse-band to storm through the room,
Clara – thinking she's done for – is about to cry
When a sudden soldier appears to shield her from doom.

It's Kracko, the Captain, now grown to a man:
He summons his toy-soldier-army to fight,
They pull out their swords as quick as they can
And go at the mouse desperados with might.

The room is still full of gifts and decorations, even though the evil mouse-army has come to spoil the fun. Add the stickers to the scene.

The brave Kracko fights with the courage of ten,
The Mouse King is losing and ready to drop;
When, tripped from behind, Kracko falls and then
In a second the Mouse King is laughing on top.

He lifts up his sword to stab Kracko dead;
Clara pulls off her shoe – something has to be done! –
She aims it and throws at the back of his head
It's a hit! The mouse drops, and the battle is won!

*Add your stickers of Clara's shoe, the Mouse King's sword and
the other items to the room.*

"You saved me, my mistress, and won us the fight!"
Says Kracko, the Prince, as he takes Clara's hand,
"You shall come with me now to be honoured this night,
By my mother, the Queen, in a faraway land".

They set off at once in a walnut-shell boat
On a bubbling ocean; when Clara exclaimed
"What's this? How can our little boat stay afloat?"
The Prince laughs and says, "the sea's pure lemonade!"

There are stickers to add to this sea scene; can you find the flying fish?

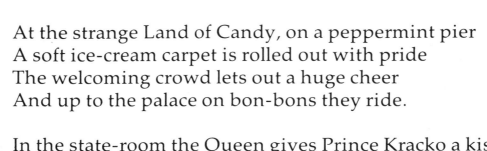

At the strange Land of Candy, on a peppermint pier
A soft ice-cream carpet is rolled out with pride
The welcoming crowd lets out a huge cheer
And up to the palace on bon-bons they ride.

In the state-room the Queen gives Prince Kracko a kiss
And squeezes dear Clara, and asks her to stay –
"I know that you saved him, my pretty young Miss,
So my kingdom is yours for a year and a day."

Here is the wonderful Land of Candy. Add the stickers of the candy-floss cloud, candy flag and other things to the picture.

Then candy-floss banners are waved through the hall,
The tables are cleared of their oceans of food,
And Sugar Plum Fairy, the belle of the ball,
Commences her dance in a magical mood.

Her dance has beauty and passion and style,
Expressing enchantment, from toe-tip to face,
And Clara is awed by her poise all the while,
By her movements and charm and her effortless grace.

*Place on your special celebration stickers in this splendid
ballroom scene.*

The Queen says to Clara "You must know my dear
That we don't exchange presents as in your land:
Instead we are granted just once every year
By the fairies, a wish, so choose something grand."

"Oh Queen I would want to be given the chance
Now I've seen how the Sugar Plum Fairy is blessed
For a night with Prince Kracko to share every dance,
With a rose in my hair and my head on his chest".

Her wish being granted, the young couple rise
And dance the most wonderful ballet of all,
Gazing alone into each other's eyes
The courtiers had faded, it seemed, and the hall.

The dance room is full of the most wonderful flowers and candies
– can you add them to the picture?

Then suddenly Clara wakes up with a start
In the room of her home, tucked up on a chair;
Was she dreaming? But here is a rose by her heart,
And close by her hand is Prince Kracko, still there . . .

*Here is Clara back in her own room, with all her things around
her. Add your stickers to this final scene.*

THE STORY OF CHRISTMAS

The story of Christmas begins with two young people called Mary and Joseph. They lived two thousand years ago in the town of Nazareth, in the country of Israel. Joseph was a carpenter. He and Mary were engaged to be married.

The Romans ruled Israel. This angered many people, but Joseph and Mary put their faith in God.

Then something extraordinary happened. Mary was sitting quietly one day, when suddenly a bright, golden light filled her room. An angel stood before her.

'Do not be afraid,' the angel said. 'I bring you good news. You have been chosen by God to be the mother of the Saviour.'

'The Saviour who was promised us?' asked Mary, amazed. 'Yes,' replied the angel Gabriel, 'and his name shall be Jesus.'

Joseph and Mary were married. The Romans then ordered a census. The people had to be counted so that they could be taxed. Everyone was to return to their place of birth. Joseph and Mary had to travel many miles to Joseph's home town, Bethlehem.

The journey was long and tiring. Mary rode on a donkey through the fields of corn and Joseph led the way. At long last they arrived at Bethlehem. The narrow streets were crowded with people who had come for the census. The little white-washed houses were filled with visitors. Joseph was worried. Mary was due to have her baby soon.

'Where shall we sleep?' asked Mary.

'It is so crowded,' sighed Joseph. 'Wait, there is an inn over there. I shall ask if they have a room.'

The innkeeper laughed.

'Have you seen how many people there are? There is no room at the inn.' And he turned away.

'My wife is about to have a baby,' said Joseph. 'We can sleep anywhere.' The innkeeper was a kind man, in spite of his gruff manner. He shrugged his shoulders.

'There is plenty of clean straw in the stable, if that will suit you. There is nothing else.'

The innkeeper led Joseph and Mary to the stable. It was warm and dry. The animals stood peacefully in the shadows. They had worked hard all day. The only sound that broke the silence was their shuffling in the straw and their deep sighs as they settled for the night.

On a lonely hill near Bethlehem there were shepherds. They were far away from the bustle of the town. Every night they watched over their sheep and kept them safe.

On this night the shepherds sat watching the stars. Suddenly, the night sky was filled with a bright light.

'Do not be afraid,' said a voice. 'I bring you tidings of great joy. The Saviour is born. He lies in a manger in Bethlehem this very night.'

The shepherds heard heavenly music, then the night sky returned to its darkness.

The shepherds stared at each other open-mouthed.

'Let us go and pay the new Saviour homage,' said one at last.

And the shepherds walked quickly down the hill into Bethlehem.

Out in the wilderness there were three other people
making a long journey. They came all the way from
Persia, and were the Magi or the Three Wise Men. These
men studied the stars and believed they could foretell
the future. One day, they saw a bright new star.

'This is the sign we have been looking for,' said one of
the Wise Men. 'The new king is soon to be born.'

'We must follow the star and pay our respects to him,'
said another.

The Wise Men left everything behind them to follow the new star. They loaded their camels with supplies and precious gifts for the Saviour. For a long time they followed the dusty trails across the deserts of Arabia. Eventually they came to Jerusalem.

Inside the ancient town walls of Bethlehem there was much excitement. People filled the narrow streets and gathered in groups. The great news was spreading. The bright star hung over the stable where Jesus lay. Outside the stable a crowd had gathered. The Wise Men made their way there. The shepherds were waiting outside. A bright light shone through the rug at the door. The people waited silently.

Joseph stepped out. He pulled the rug aside. Quietly and timidly the visitors stepped into the warmth of the stable.

Inside sat the new mother, Mary. She looked happy and peaceful. Behind her, the silent oxen were kneeling as if in prayer. The visitors stepped forward nervously. They knelt down and offered their gifts to the baby Jesus.

The shepherds gave the child a lamb that they had brought with them. The Wise Men placed gently beside the manger their gifts of Gold, Frankincense and Myrrh. Then they bowed their heads and worshipped the New King.

Mary wrapped the baby Jesus in linen and laid him in the manger to sleep. She smiled at him as she rocked him gently. It was the first Christmas Day.

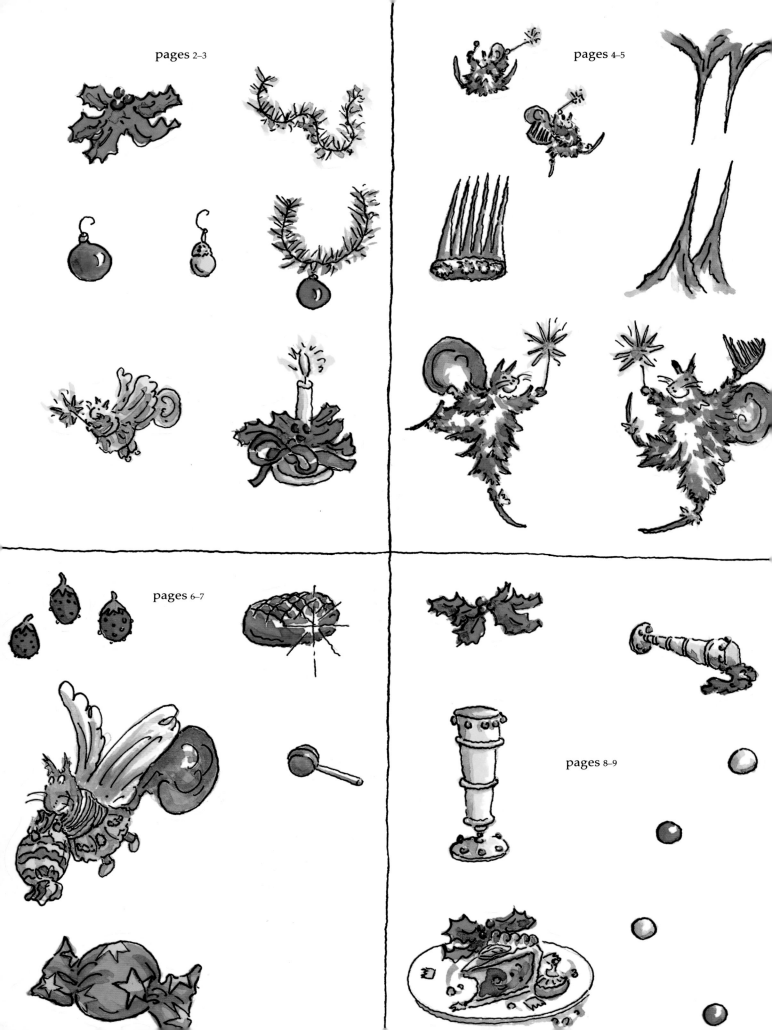

pages 2–3

pages 4–5

pages 6–7

pages 8–9

pages 10–11

pages 12–13

pages 14–15

page 16

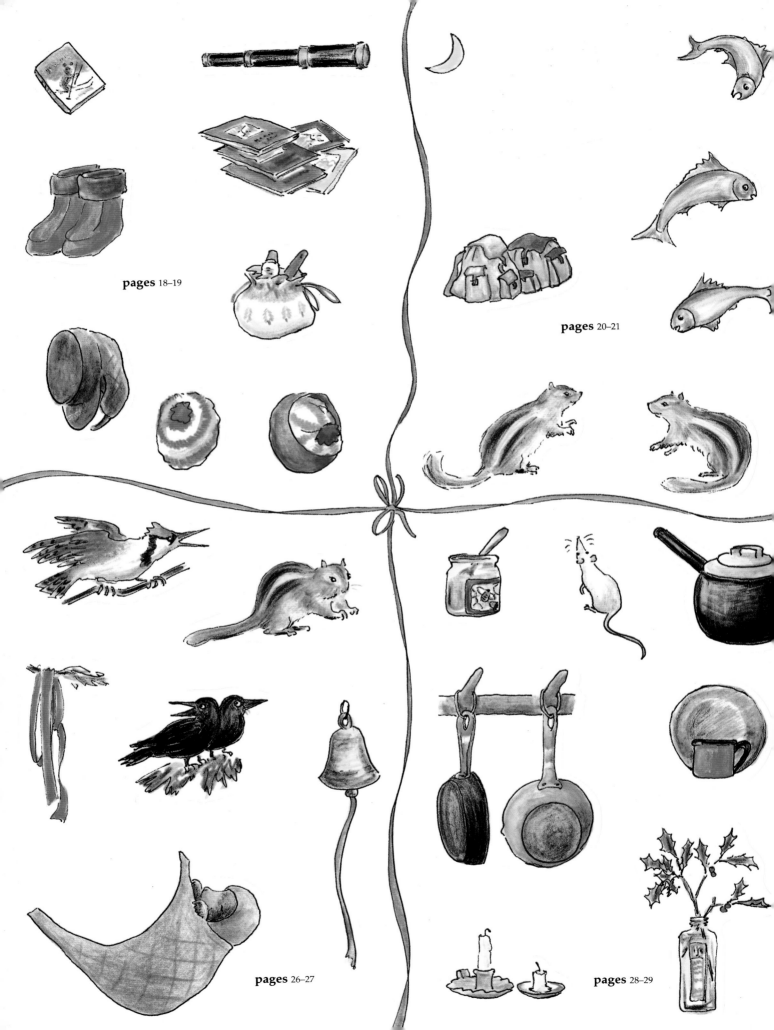

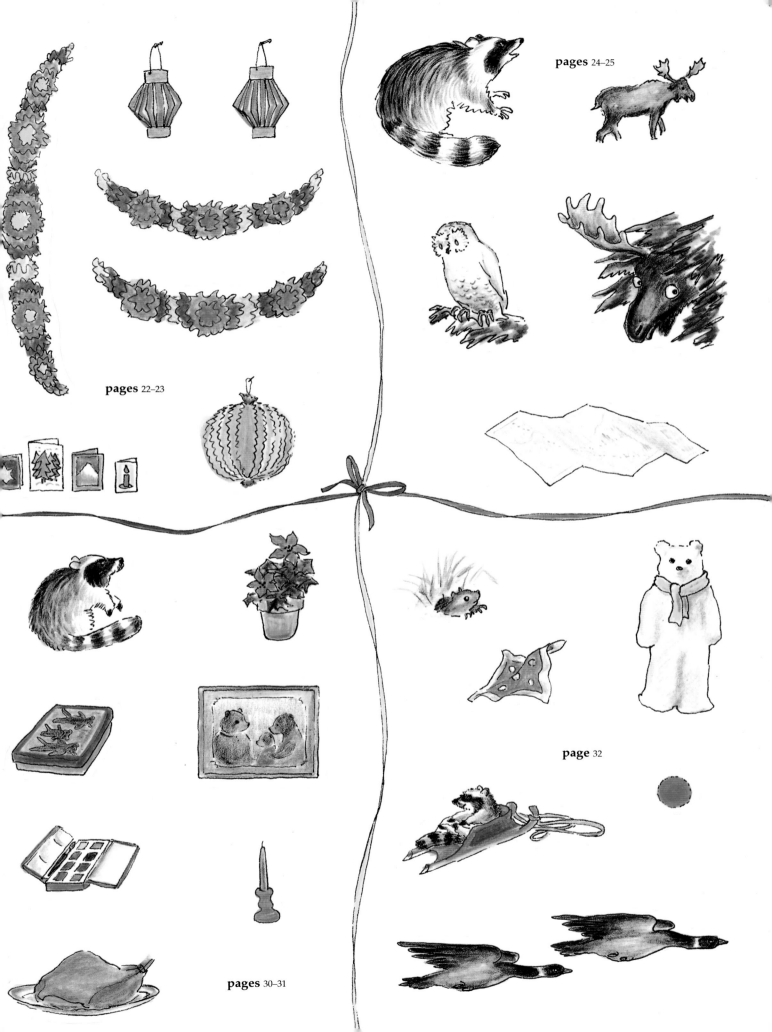

pages 22–23

pages 24–25

page 32

pages 30–31

pages 34–35

pages 36–37

pages 42–43

pages 44–45

pages 38–39

page 40

page 41

pages 46–47

page 48

page 49

page 64

pages 50–51

pages 52–53

pages 54–55

pages 56–57

pages 58–59

pages 60–61

pages 62–63